The Blue Book of Poetry

Gwynne Gladden

THE BLUE BOOK OF POETRY
Copyright © 1997 by Gwynne Gladden

ALL RIGHTS RESERVED
This book may not be reproduced in whole or in part,
by mimeograph or any other means, without permission.

ISBN 1-57579-090-4

Printed in the United States of America

PINE HILL PRESS, INC.
Freeman, S. Dak. 57029

Table of Contents

Poem   Page

Introduction *1*
Seasons *2*
Rain *3*
Dragonfly *4*
Amber *5*
Tuna *6*
Grandmother's Rooster *7*
The Mockingbird *8*
Toad *9*
Visitor in My Garden *10*
Kitty Fern *11*
My Cedar Tree *12*
Solitude *13*
Window Shopping *14*
Patriotism *15*
Teachers *16*
The Crusader *17*
Time *18*
Victory's Seeds *19*
Optimism *20*
Garden Hoses *21*
Oak Wood *22*
A Spy Called Riley *23*
To Doctors *24*
Driving *25*
Automobiles *26*
Computers *27*
Halloween *28*
The Chattanooga 630 .... *29*
The Psyche *30*
Our Secret Garden *31*
Noah's Ark *32*
Jerusalem *33*
Life's Road *34*

*To my mother
Marguerite Ming
and to Dr. Tamara Miller
for their inspiration.*

Introduction

It is hoped that these poems you have bought,
Will entertain and give you cause for thought.

So, please take a look inside this blue book,
May these poems be worth the time you took.

Seasons

Summer on her golden slippered feet,
Comes to my garden as Spring retreats.

She paints my landscape a verdant hue,
Underneath a sky of cerulean blue.

And for a while she rules my bower,
Sure of her grand and vibrant power.

But Summer like the small, dappled fawn,
She does not remain in one place long.

Then away Summer takes her artist's easel.
Next comes Autumn fast as a weasel.

Scatters her fiery hues on my grounds,
Then takes her pallet to other towns.

Last comes Winter, and with great delight
He paints my lawn titanium white.

Rain

Like heartfelt tears the stormy sky,
Drops her rain while safe in bed I lie.

The countless drops of shimmering rain,
Beat a tattoo on my weather vane.

The rain whirls about on my rooftop,
And moves on without wanting to stop.

Down it flows to the streets and gutters,
Then forms streamlets that dance and flutter.

The streamlets spill into large storm drains,
And on they go through the water mains.

Next into streams the rain water pours,
Then onward to the broad river floors.

Down rivers the rain water then soars,
Until it raps at the ocean's door.

Dragonfly

The dragonfly's an ancient friend.
On jewel wings he dips and bends.

Flies daintily in summer skies.
He views the world through primal eyes.

To a water world he is born,
But can't remain an aquatic form.

His adulthood is spent on land.
His changing life is nature's plan.

The "darning needle", he is called,
Because he is slim over-all.

I'd like to be a fairy queen,
And ride some dragonfly I deem.

But dragonflies can't be ridden,
Though in print it's not forbidden.

Amber

I had a small, brown dog named Amber.
She was fat and round like a panda.

She had small white feet and perky eyes.
She could hunt and my cats thought her wise.

Amber stopped my cats from having fights.
She kept the peace; what she did was right.

Amber played with a great many toads.
She was often found digging for moles.

Her life was long; I am happy to write.
And I still love her with all my might.

Tuna

My cats want their tuna,
   but the vet tells me to say no.
A balanced diet he claims
   is the only way to go.

My tabbies dismiss his orders
   with a wave of their tails,
For their own supermarkets
   can be found on every trail.

Lots of tuna and some birds
   will surely meet all their needs.
That is what my cats have told me
   while hunting through my weeds.

Grandmother's Rooster

My grandmother's rooster woke up the new day.
He came from her hen house not too far away.

Soldier-like he marched to the front of her house.
His mind was on crowing, not on some ole mouse.

He jumped up on a post and let out his call.
Yes, dawn was a good time to rise one and all!

He gave forth his song with a hint of some rhyme.
Although he sang only five notes at a time.

My grandmother's rooster had comical ways.
He brings back dear memories of bygone days.

The Mockingbird

The mockingbird he chases the crow.
Back and forth in the sky they go.

The mockingbird he flies supreme.
He's captain of the sky it seems.

The hawk appears and changes take place.
High in a tree the crow is safe.

Gone from the crow, the mocker hides.
He fears the hawk who spies and glides.

Toad

There's a toad in my yard, I'm glad to say.
He eats bugs and worms, when they come his way.

This toad of mine sleeps quite late in the day.
Don't hold him or warts you will get they say.

He sleeps under rocks and anywhere cool.
This toad has brains; he ain't anyone's fool.

When winter comes my toad can not be found.
Toad has dug a hole deep down in the ground.

He's buried as if dead all winter long.
Toad doesn't emerge till the sun shines strong.

I like my toad; he is special to me.
I could be wrong, but I think he's a he.

Although lowly in state, as deemed by man,
To God and to me he's a worthy plan.

Visitor in My Garden

I was pounding some stakes in the ground,
When I was startled by rustling sounds.

Eyes burning bright as a beam of light,
Stared back at me six feet to my right.

It was a snake in my iris bed,
Oh yes, I saw his bright, greenish head.

He stuck out his tongue and smelled the air.
I moved not an inch, I would not dare.

Then to my great relief and delight,
Suddenly, that snake was gone from sight.

Kitty Fern

My little furry jungle queen,
Cast out your most fanciful dreams.

Transport yourself way back in time,
Before the first dawn of mankind.

When man's dominion had no form,
And cats roamed freely, was the norm.

Man's callous laws have hemmed you in.
Man's disregard for you, his sin.

Yet through dreams you may glimpse the past.
Return to domains ever vast.

My Cedar Tree

A silhouette against the night sky,
My cedar rises thirty feet high.

Straight she stands in my garden green.
She grows not far from an ancient stream.

Dances sprightly with the passing winds,
She moves with grace as she twists and bends.

Many birds seek her branches for rest,
And in summer she hides the dove's nest.

The small hummingbird flies to my tree,
Gets spider webs for her nest so wee.

Solitude

Sometimes when I sit motionless and all alone,
My dauntless imagination makes herself known.

Then Solitude with her gentle and quiet grace,
Takes me daydreaming at a calm and measured pace.

She leads me where my thoughts can soar with boundless flight,
And I can banish life's contentions from my sight.

Solitude brings great comfort and peace to my mind.
She has brought me inspiration from time to time.

May I continue to partake of dreamer's food,
When my imagination walks with Solitude.

Window Shopping

I'm the kind of person who'd rather window shop, not buy.
What is the point of shopping when the prices are so high!

I pause at each shop's window to see what items are for sale,
Then on to more awaiting stores I will happily sail.

What I see in the department stores is mine, I pretend.
Maybe I'll be lucky and get what I like in the end.

My vicarious way of shopping is the way to shop,
For what I spend are just my dreams, of which I have a lot.

Patriotism

Has our patriotism been destroyed by our greed?
Will selfishness and indifference be our creed?

Will we let crime and terrorism blight our fair land?
Do we have any respect for an honest man?

As citizens, do we owe our great country naught?
For our homeland are we doing all that we ought?

Our nation has nurtured us and brought us much wealth.
Her protection has provided us with good health.

Forget not our pledge of allegiance to our flag,
So that patriotism in this land will not lag!

Teachers

Some teachers grade and some teachers teach.
They are unlike each other I preach.

The first lacks compassion you must see.
The second has mercy that's the key.

Merciful teachers are not judgmental you see.
So be not quick to judge your students I pray thee.

Take heed you teacher that would label a child dumb.
For more likely than not a dunce he will become.

The Crusader

The Arabian horse and the crescent sword,
Were more than a match for the crusader horde.

With his heavy armor and long-waisted horse,
The crusader appeared quite clumsy of course.

His sword weighed too much and took time to unsheath.
When ready, his head was often at his feet.

The heat was more than the crusader could bear.
Why did he have armor he hated to wear?

Some crusaders were lucky and got back home.
But for many, their fate will remain unknown.

Time

The eternal beat of passing time,
Has cast a shadow on all mankind.

Though time's with me every place I go,
I find time can often be my foe.

So often I don't get the leisure,
To do the things that give me pleasure.

But time creeps by for many an hour,
When I have a job that makes me sour.

Now time has not always caused me strife,
Time's left me happy thoughts from my life.

Clear are my memories saved from time,
When youth's bright promises were once mine.

Victory's Seeds

The seeds of victory are within us all.
Unnoticed they wait only for hope's bright call.

Have courage now, all who feel beaten by time;
Those shamed by the proud man with a clever mind.

You can be victorious with joyous hope.
Sing with gladness and give forth a happy note.

Victory's seeds can burst the bonds of failure.
Your life can bloom lovely like an azalea.

Optimism

Let your optimism get the better of you,
Else you'll never try many things you'd like to do.

Don't let discouragement breed pessimistic lies.
Dreams often become reality when you try.

Don't tremble at the thought of reaching for a star.
It's not as hard to do as it seems from afar.

With optimism as your guide, your life will take on hope.
You can with hope throw off ole fatalism's cloak.

Garden Hoses

Garden hoses are waiting to get you, if they can.
They have but one sly and infamous plan.

To leave you soaking wet, is their burning desire.
What do they think they're doing, putting out a fire?

They will spring a leak in the blink of an eye.
Don't try to repair them; just kiss them good-bye.

They are hard to coil and get in the way.
I wish from my yard, garden hoses would stay.

Oak Wood

Houses today are built of soft lumber,
So fires quickly devour them no wonder.

In frontier days houses were built from oaks.
These were the homes of our pioneer folks.

Their homes were strong and many still can be seen,
Through this land of the American dream.

People say soft lumber is the best to use,
But you won't find soft wood made into church pews.

If you think soft wood is better than hard oak,
Try and drive a nail into a piece of oak.

A Spy Called Riley

There was once a very clever spy called Riley.
His enemies thought him ruthless, bold and wily.

He was a double agent and his work had flair.
Riley wouldn't hesitate to act on a dare.

He spied for the English and the Russians as well.
It's no telling how many spies he caused to fail.

He disappeared one day from his English dwelling.
What happened to Riley, it's really no telling.

Did he boast in Russia that the English he'd tamed?
Did he meet with misfortune or win at this game?

To Doctors

Doctors please drop your stethoscope, clip board and pen,
And read this poem of mine to the very end!

You hurry about in your starched jacket of white,
All through the long day and well into the dark night.

Now slow down! You can certainly get it all done,
Just don't examine patient one hundred and one.

All day you write prescriptions in mystical script.
So it's no wonder that you are lacking some wit.

Trying to keep track of patients, staff and what all,
Must leave you quite mad and almost ready to bawl.

You take the old Hippocratic oath to heal all.
So when was the last time that you made a house call?

Your bills appear designed for Kuwaiti princes.
If you lower your bills you could mend fences.

It's true you know a lot, but you don't know it all.
Your ego could cause you to trip and take a fall.

When a nurse acts stupid, don't give her a mean look.
Why even Einstein once lost a check in some book.

Now please do not take what you have read here to heart.
This poem was not written with ill will on my part.

It should really not hurt to poke a little fun,
At you doctors as long as no harm has been done.

Driving

I was driving down the highway on a hot summer day.
There was nothing on my mind and I had nothing to say.

I passed a little, red Jeep looking mighty, mighty sweet.
A gold Cadillac waltzed by and my heart fell at its feet.

I noticed a lady with a brown, curly head of hair,
And you could tell she had combed it with a great deal of care.

Well now, it turned out the lady was no lady at all.
She was just a brown poodle sitting very straight and tall.

On to the interstate I went without a bit of glee.
I drove on forever with cars on either side of me.

I couldn't find my exit; it was playing hide and seek.
Getting lost in traffic can leave even the mighty meek!

So, I drove around and around till my exit I found.
Finally arrived at my destination safe and sound.

Automobiles

Automobiles on fast moving wheels, are everywhere.
They are nasty beasts, and I find them quite hard to bear.

Cars play dead, if you ever forget to give them gas.
Feed them lots of gasoline and in the sun they bask.

They are just waiting to lead you into the deep woods,
With their Chinese puzzles lying down under their hoods.

Cars are money spenders, they can't ever get enough.
Tell them to economize and they get mighty tough.

They will at once start to whine, thump, rattle, ping and click.
They are showing you there's something wrong, and they are sick.

Quickly to the mechanic you are then forced to go.
The mechanic will be waiting to take all your dough.

Since cars first appeared they have been a financial drain,
Yet without these overpriced machines our lives would wane.

Computers

You must know now
   that the computer age is definitely here.
It has changed our lives for the better,
   so you need not have fear.

Inside each microcomputer
   a silicon chip is placed.
It handles data without making mistakes;
   it won't lose face.

On each chip are small transistors
   which will quickly work for you.
They help the computers carry out
   many a job on cue.

Computers are really adding machines,
   believe it or not.
Because of their nature, in the business world
   they have got their slot.

They can subtract, multiply and divide
   with a speed that pays,
Just by adding plus and minus values
   in various ways.

Halloween

On mystical, magical Halloween night,
Little ghosts and goblins may give you a fright.

Witches on their mothers' brooms,
Fly about before the moon.

"Trick or treat", these small ones cry,
Then they are gone in the blink of an eye.

The Chattanooga 630

The click of the rails has a rhythm that prevails,
As ole 630 hits the Chattanooga trail.

She's a steam locomotive and she's still in use.
She glides on ribbons made of steel when she's turned loose.

Come climb to her cabin and pull her steel throttle.
Blow her whistle for she is no disused model.

The Psyche

What is the essence of a man?
What causes him to form his plans?

We can not use measures or weights,
To shed light on a person's traits.

Psyche profiles, we often show.
But only God our soul can know.

Our Secret Garden

In everyone a secret garden dwells.
Oh that we all would try hard to tend it well!

Nurture it with kind, wise and noble thoughts.
Plant many seeds of hope, as we all ought.

For in this secret garden abides man's soul;
It is his very essence we are told.

Keep this garden from harm's way while you can.
Remember numbered are the days of man.

Noah's Ark

Way, way back in biblical times God spoke to Noah's heart.
God said he had a plan for him and he must build an ark.

Noah built the ark for God furnished him with the know how.
He took on his ark many animals both beast and fowl.

It's thought Noah's ark was four hundred and fifty feet long.
It must have been built by many men both clever and strong.

This great and wondrous vessel stood forty-five feet tall.
Noah water-proofed it by brushing pitch on each wall.

When the rain came down, Noah on his journey did embark.
Now, Noah floated for many months safe within his ark.

Once back on dry land a covenant Noah did receive.
A covenant God promised to keep which Noah believed.

God said there would never again be floods like this on earth.
The rainbow's a reminder of this promise and its worth.

Jerusalem

The city of Jerusalem,
 now the capital of Israel,
Has long been a favorite subject
 of a many a biblical tale.

There are many ties that bind
 the Christian faith to this old city.
Here King David ruled
 and Jesus showed the money changers no pity.

Nebuchadnezzar, Pompey and Saladin
 for this city fought.
And on this very day enmity remains
 though peace is being sought.

Life's Road

Lord let me not be weary
   of life's journey I must take.
Let me be strong when from stress and sorrow
   There seems no break.

May I walk with hope's promise
   down the straight and narrow road.
May my burdens be removed
   so I'll feel no heavy load.